Living a Blessed Life

By Grant Virtue

ISBN-13: 978-0615579436 (Virtue Press)

ISBN-10: 0615579434

To my wife, without whom all of my blessings would be meaningless.

Contents

Introduction

You may be asking yourself, "What is a blessed life anyway?" It is different to each of us, but if you think about it for any length of time, you will most likely find that you already know the answer. A blessed life is the life that you have always dreamed about, even at those times when dreaming seemed futile.

A blessed life is a life filled with love, abundance, joy, and a total lack of want. It does not necessarily mean that you will be a millionaire, although that is not out of reach for anyone. It also does not necessarily mean that you will be married, have two and one-half children, a golden retriever, a minivan, and a two-story home. While having all of those things is certainly a remarkable blessing in some people's lives, it is not considered an ideal by everyone.

Your life is now, as it always has been, yours to make of it what you want. I simply offer these steps that you can do right now, which can help bring you to that place where your life is truly blessed and as you have always wanted it to be. Every one of these tips is nondenominational.

Each can be tailored to suit your life, to be utilized when it is needed and ignored when it is not. No one but you is monitoring your progress, and no one will be disappointed in you if you slip up from time to time.

If you choose to follow these steps, then you will be taking an active role in improving your situation daily. You will be a cocreator in your bliss and your life, and you will be able to tailor each situation to what you want it to be. No longer will you be reacting to the world around you, but you will be the force to which your surroundings react.

Throughout this book I will present you with the method that works very effectively in my life and the lives of those people I am lucky enough to spend my time with. Of course, I do not follow every single one of these steps every single day. I skip, forget, or just plain ignore each of them from time to time. However, when I do skip them I notice a marked decrease in my level of happiness.

Sometimes I forget that these steps are not a burden placed here to make my life harder but the reason my life is so good in the first place.

But, like everyone else, I am only human. And as a human, the most stubborn of creatures, I will continuously forget and relearn these lessons for the rest of my natural life. I do not feel ashamed of this; and, if for some reason you find yourself doing the same thing, I ask that you also feel no shame. It simply is part of the great learning process of life.

Each of our lives is our own to live. Now go out and make yours the life you have always wanted.

Chapter 1

Forgive

I have listed forgiveness as the first of these steps for a very important reason: it is the most important. Anyone would find it difficult to lead a blessed life while carrying around the very large burden of blame and anger. It is essential for your well-being to learn how to forgive and forget.

The act of forgiveness in no way says that the other person was in the right. It does not mean that what the person did was okay or that he or she is welcome to do it again. Above all forgiveness does not mean you have to be around that person in any capacity or even speak to him or her. You do not even need to let the person know he or she is forgiven.

Why? While forgiveness may be the greatest gift ever given, you are giving it to yourself. For the most part, holding a grudge does not affect the other person all that much. It has a far greater effect on you if you let yourself hold on to the anger and resentment perhaps for years.

Think of the last time someone made you angry. It could be a person who cut you off on the highway, someone trying to cheat you, or any other person who did something that raised your hackles. How did it feel when you were angry? Now think how it felt when you realized that you were no longer angry. For most of us, that feeling is akin to removing a very large burden from our back. This is essentially what forgiveness is; it is taking the burden of anger from your back and allowing yourself to return to being happy.

For the most part, anger and happiness are mutually exclusive states of being. You may be able to forget for a time that you are angry, but sooner or later something will remind you of the person or situation that has upset you. This is like living with a time bomb, one that you alone can disarm. However, until you disarm it, it can go off at any moment and obliterate any feelings of happiness. Obviously it should be an important goal of yours to remove this burden as soon as possible.

I am not saying that the emotions of anger, resentment, or wounded pride are invalid or unwelcome. I am not suggesting that if you have these feelings something may be wrong with you. You are a free person and no one is trying to change you. However, I have seen the results up close and personal of living a life filled with anger and a lack of forgiveness. It is not pretty or pleasant to be around.

These emotions are not something you should live with. Rather, they are to be seen, recognized, and allowed to pass over and through you. Holding on to them serves no larger purpose than holding on to a smoldering log. You must release them or risk being burned.

"How is one to forgive?" you may ask. Fortunately this is very easy. Depending on your religious background, you may have some more or less complicated rituals associated with laying down the burden of blame; but for the most part it is simply recognition within yourself.

You can recognize that holding on to anger, resentment, and the desire to punish someone is only hurting yourself. You can recognize that the person you have yet to forgive may not even be aware that you are holding him or her in such contempt. Or if the person does know, it is entirely possible and even probable that he or she does not care. If you are the only one being harmed by the grudge, then you owe it to yourself to let it go and forgive.

Again, this does not mean you approve of what happened or welcome it to happen again. It only means that you are freeing yourself from this person and allowing the pain to stop. However, for this to work you do have to truly forgive him or her. Nobody is checking your progress; so if you are still holding on to anger, then you are only cheating yourself out of the healing that you so dearly deserve. Often forgiveness can be an ongoing process, and you may have to work at it for some time before it finally takes.

One advantage people with strong spiritual backgrounds have is that forgiveness comes more naturally to them. They recognize that we are all children put here to learn and that sometimes we make mistakes. Often those mistakes hurt other people, but for what other purpose were we put here on Earth but to learn from those mistakes and try not to repeat them? Certainly it sometimes appears as if a particular person or group of people have no intention of correcting or learning from their mistakes, and that they seem bent on making the same ones over and over again much to everyone else's dismay.

What is important in this case is to again see them as merely children trying to learn the best way they can, and to at least distance yourself from them so they cannot harm you with their behavior. This distancing does not mean that you are angry with them or hold them to a special sort of guilt; it simply means that you accept them for who they are but must protect yourself and your loved ones from them.

I was recently given an opportunity to relearn this lesson. Some years back I met a man under very unfortunate circumstances. This man had some troubles of his own, but I was led to believe he was safe to be around. Suffice it to say that he was not and my family was put in a highly dangerous situation as a result.

I had held on to a very strong anger toward this man and tried my best to avoid him. However someone I know very well and trusted implicitly chose to involve herself with this very same man recently. Suddenly I was a wreck! I was devastated by the thought that I had been deceived and betrayed by someone I truly believed was as driven to protect me as I was to protect her.

Then it hit me. I was not angry at this man for his misbehavior. I didn't know him or even care enough about him to be angry with him. The person I was really angry with was me for letting him become a threat in the first place and my dear friend for bringing him back into my family's life.

This, I believe, highlights some of the danger of not forgiving. My anger was so reckless and blind that all this time I had thought I was upset with this man. I could not truly forgive him because I was never angry at him in the first place. Until I could find the real targets of my anger, I could not let it go.

I have since forgiven myself and my friend for that long-ago situation. I am no longer carrying that heavy burden of blame and anger. I recognize that my friend did not intentionally set out to betray me any more than that man set out to intentionally put my family in danger. They, like all of us, were simply doing what they thought was best for them at the time.

Ideally you would be able to make peace with the people you are forgiving and not have to distance yourself from them. Unfortunately this is not always possible, but it remains something to strive toward.

We will leave this first step with one final thought: The best gift you will ever give or receive is forgiveness.

Chapter 2

Exercise

That noise you just heard was a collective groan from all the other readers of this chapter. Nobody likes to think about exercise because we all know we need to do more of it. I know all the excuses because I have used them myself. Yes, making time for exercise can be a challenge at first. I am aware that some of the people in the gym can seem rather unpleasant for a variety of reasons, and I can think of fifteen other things I'd rather be doing as well.

However, that does not change the fact that we need to exercise. It does not matter how hard you exercise but how often and for how long. A thirty-minute walk each day is plenty for some people. This can be just a simple stroll through your neighborhood in the morning or after you get back from work. It is better than nothing, costs nothing, and can easily be incorporated into a busy lifestyle if you find a nearby grocery store or post office and make that your destination.

The great Jewish philosopher Maimonides said it best when he stated, "The well-being of the soul can only be obtained after that of the body has been secured."

A little thinking on this statement reveals the wisdom it contains. After all, how motivated can a person be to improve his or her spiritual situation if he or she fears for his or her health? Because our time on this planet is limited and because the length of time we have is in direct correlation to the health of our body, it stands to reason that we first take care of our body in order to give ourselves time to take care of our mind and spirit.

This is step number two and no farther down the list because simple, light exercise can help you to concentrate better, feel better, sleep better, and just be able to cope with life better. Sometimes this world can be a bit tough, so we need to strengthen ourselves.

You do not necessarily have to become a gym person, and how much you exercise is up to you. But many people find that the more they exercise, the more they love it and want to do more. This is fine. However, if you find a very simple routine and want to stick with it, that is just fine, too.

I would like to take this opportunity to mention that nothing in this step relates to weight. Your weight is your own business. You should not let anyone make you feel bad about your appearance any more than you would let someone abuse you about any other aspect of your life. This chapter is simply about health.

It is possible, and I have known many people who fit the bill, to exercise every single day and not shed a pound. In fact, because muscle does weigh more than fat, some people find that they gain weight once they start exercising regularly. This is not something to panic about, and you shouldn't let it discourage you. We are not setting up a diet here, merely another daily habit to make you feel better. Pay no attention to the scale, and just go by what makes you feel good.

Once you start a simple exercise routine, you may notice how much you enjoy it. Most people I know who exercise regularly begin not to even pay attention to the fact that they are exercising. They use that time to free their minds of the usual constraints and pressures that they face. When you are exercising, you truly are free to just be you; no one can possibly expect you to do anything else at that moment. As in the previous chapter, where we discussed how following that step is a gift to yourself, this step of exercise is a gift that you have earned and deserve.

You may be thinking that I'd have to be daft to consider exercise a gift. Trust me, it quickly becomes one. The payoffs of longevity, health, and happiness are yours and yours alone. You will find yourself smiling a lot more; and, perhaps most remarkable, people who take this small step toward becoming healthier tend to take it a bit further.

For example, it would not be out of the ordinary for someone to take up light jogging and after a while suddenly quit smoking. Perhaps this person had never considered giving up the habit before, but now the jogging has become more important than the cigarettes. I have also known people who started recreational lap swimming and then quit drinking alcohol, which had weakened the individual's muscles to a dangerous level.

If this sounds like a daunting prospect to you, then simplify it. If you would only commit to exercise three days a week for one month and then see how you feel, I can virtually guarantee that you will not want to go back.

Again, nobody is checking on your progress, so there is no reason to feel bad or guilty if you do not make your goal. However, if you do not make it, I do encourage you to keep trying and not give up. This one very simple step will help you live longer and give you more time to live the blessed life you have always wanted. Plus you will feel so good that you will enjoy those extra years far more than you can imagine now.

Chapter 3

Pray

This is a very fortunate time to be alive because, after a century-long schism, spirituality and science are once again beginning to reconcile their differences. Both the new spiritual teachers and some particularly enlightened scientists are starting to realize that they are both saying the same thing, just in different ways.

Not all that long ago in the course of human development, it would have been a very rare case for a doctor or scientist not to acknowledge the hand of our creator in the human body and our natural world. That eventually changed when the atheist movement sprang up rather suddenly. While that movement is still unfortunately going strong, we are at last seeing a reversal of that trend in scientists themselves.

Studies on prayer have been conducted in fairly rapid-fire succession in recent years. Larry

Dossey, MD, author of such works as *The Extraordinary Healing Power of Ordinary Things*, has this to say on the subject: "In 1993, only three U.S. medical schools had courses devoted to exploring the role of religious practice and prayer in health; currently 80 medical schools have instituted such courses."

It is far safer to say that it is proven fact, rather than mere theory, that prayer can and does have an enormous positive impact on our lives. You may have seen the results of a couple of studies on prayer that stated there was no effect at all, or worse that prayer seemed to cause harm to the person who was praying. The fact is that there is a tremendous difference between cold mechanical prayer and genuine, devoted, and heartfelt praying. As in all other areas of our lives, we cannot simply go at this halfheartedly and expect dramatic results.

Whom or what you pray to does not matter as much as people might think. A person's beliefs are his or her own to nurture and understand. I do not seek to convert anyone to my religious views just as I try my best to avoid those who would try to convert me.

Each of us is wise in our own heart as to how we prefer to express our devotion in recognition of a higher power. I do not believe that our creator is all that interested in what particular name we choose to call Him, much the same as any other aspect of nature is content to be named as humans see fit. To give the burden of jealousy to a deity is to bring it down to a very human level.

Likewise how you pray is not all that important so long as it is meaningful to you. Every major religion has its own particular way to pray, even if most members of those groups choose to disregard those particular ways. Each way is valid, and any way that you have come up with on your own is also valid. As long as you are performing the act in a very sincere and genuine way you will see a result.

The great thing about prayer is that you have nothing to lose by trying it. The act itself takes but moments, is socially acceptable enough that you do not have to make special provisions to perform it, and can be done at any time of the day or night. You can pray for anything and anyone, for yourself, or just in general without having to perform any special ceremonies or complicated rituals.

At that moment you are just speaking to your creator in the best way you know how. You need not tell anyone what you are doing. You especially do not need to tell anyone whom you are praying to and in which manner.

Of course group prayer has its exponential benefits; so if you can find other like-minded individuals to pray with, so much the better. However, if you are in doubt about how someone will react to your telling them about your prayer practices, you will probably be better served by simply keeping them to yourself. This is one aspect of your life where you can certainly do without any negativity.

Some studies have shown a surprisingly large number of benefits received by people after they have prayed. Positive results have included but are not limited to reduced blood pressure, shorter post-surgery healing time, fewer medical complications in connection with autoimmune diseases, and a greatly increased resistance to illness in the first place.

What is even more remarkable about these results is that they are not seen only in the person who performs the prayer. Studies have found that an equal benefit can be found in persons who are being prayed for. This means that not only can you dramatically improve your own life through this simple and wonderful tool, but you can also make the lives of everyone around you—indeed everyone on Earth—measurably better.

Like all the steps presented to you in this small book, the best way to approach praying is to start small. If you do not already pray regularly, it can be a bit daunting to start up this new practice.

You can start by setting a small and obtainable goal for yourself, such as a resolution to pray once a week at a set time. Even if you cannot think of something to pray about when the time comes, simply by initiating the conversation with your creator you are enacting a powerful force of change upon yourself and the world. Sometimes the most effective thing you can do is to pray for nothing specific. Just by praying for universal peace, health, and abundance, you are by extension helping to heal yourself in those areas as well.

We humans have been given the wonderful gift of free will, but it needs to be used responsibly. Free will is the most amazing thing imaginable, for without it we would be nothing more than automatons going through life on the whims of fate. Even if we were capable of choice, no individual choice would matter because our life would not be our own. That would also mean that anything we learn during our brief stay on Earth would ultimately be meaningless.

Unless we are allowed to make our own mistakes and our own choices, we may as well just be asleep behind the wheel. Certainly we would be moving, but it would probably be best if we were not. Luckily that is not the case, and we have been given free will. This means that we can decide to live our lives the way we want to. The goodness that happens in our lives and the unfortunate parts as well are infinitely changeable by us. We can insert ourselves or extract ourselves from any situation that is or is not for our highest good.

Of course we are not the lone architects in our lives. While our lives are not preordained, our creator does have a divine plan and life purpose for us. We are free to disregard that plan and life purpose, usually to our own peril, but freely nonetheless. When it comes to divine intervention in our life we are equally free to ignore it or seek it out.

However, our creator cannot help us unless we ask for it. Because we have free will, we are free not to have any assistance if that is what we choose. I know some people have a very difficult time asking for help, and this practice of praying can help with that. No one is going to judge you because no one knows that you are asking. That is between you and whatever deity you wish to consult with.

Remember that every divine being you can think of is simply a facet on the diamond that is the creator, so never fear that you are praying to the wrong one. No being will be angry with you for how you choose to express your spiritual belief. This false belief that some people are unfortunately saddled with is simply a means of control and is an all-too-human attempt at understanding that which is not understandable.

To give our own limited and flawed human attributes of anger and jealousy to a perfect being is not accurate or fair. It is better to simply admit that the nature of our creator is beyond our understanding and always will be. This leaves all doors open and prevents any of us from judging another person's relationship with the divine creator.

We shall leave this step with a final thought from the great Sufi luminary and poet Jalal ad-Din Muhammad Rumi about prayer: "Listen, stand up in prayer during the night, for you are a candle, and at night a candle stands and burns."

Chapter 4

Give

Giving is one of the finest occupations a person can hope for. It may seem counterintuitive to give away money as a profession. However, it can and does make for a very worthy way to make a living. When you give, not only are you helping someone in need, but you are signifying to the universe that you are a person who will use abundance in a socially responsible manner. This does not mean that you deserve wealth any more than the next person, but it does mean that you understand the true purpose of wealth.

Wealth is earned by and bestowed upon those who can use it for the benefit of everyone. While it would be very easy to point at some self-made millionaire and suggest that he or she alone created the wealth and owes nothing to anyone, this is a very flawed way of looking at not only abundance but the world in general. Each of us is put on this Earth to achieve our life purpose, and not everyone's life purpose is to become a rich industrialist. Likewise it may seem as if this man or woman worked hard all by him- or herself to earn this money, but the truth of the matter is quite different.

Not one cent is earned without the consent of the creator. Think about this for a second because it does merit contemplation. Every dollar, pound, or euro you have or ever will earn is because the Source of all abundance has allowed you to do so. It may be considered a distasteful thing in this day and age to think that we possibly live our lives at the pleasure of someone greater than ourselves, but that does not make it any less true. Granted, the creator is absolute and without limit, so it is within the realm of possibility for everyone to earn astounding quantities of money. Yet most of us get lost and forget who the true Source is.

Often people think of their bosses, spouses, government, or family as the source of their prosperity and well-being. This simply is not accurate. The truth is that all of this belongs to your creator, who bestows wealth upon you as an act of love and trust. Because your altruistic tendency is also an act of love and trust, you attract more affluence and abundance into your life. It is the old story of like attracts like.

This step, like all the others, has a very human side to it. History and fiction are rife with stories of greedy people who gave nothing to anyone in need. More often than not, these people end up much worse off for their greed; and, in some particularly delightful stories, they realize the error of their ways. Because the distaste for greed is such a part of our culture, the act of giving naturally makes you more appealing to other people.

You may see yourself in no position to be giving anything away. You may see yourself as not all that well off financially, with far too many people dependent on you as it is. Perhaps you are just a bit jaded from seeing too many beggars in the street and can't find the energy within yourself to give more money to a seemingly lost cause. This may be true, however keep in mind that charitable organizations, animal shelters, soup kitchens, and other altruistic institutions require your time just as much as they do your funding.

Volunteering is a particularly generous way to give back to the world. It is at the volunteer level that the rubber meets the road, so to speak. While donations allow these organizations to continue their good works and have a team of dedicated volunteers, it is the volunteers themselves who have a direct hand in helping those people or creatures who are in need at that moment.

Volunteering can also lead to some surprisingly large health benefits for the volunteer. Studies have proven that volunteering as little as one hour a month leads to far fewer reported cases of depression, increased resiliency after a heart attack, and a marked reduction in the age-related decline of health and bodily function for older volunteers.

Some people may find it hard to accept the generally agreed-upon idea that you must give without thought of reward. How is this possible, given all that we know about the benefits of giving? The most effective way I have found to give without its becoming a selfish thing is to simply keep to myself what I have done and for whom.

It is easy in this age of instant connections to Facebook or Tweet about what we do for others. However, if you can resist that urge to brag about your good works, you will find that the feeling you get from performing your altruistic deeds lasts far longer than the thrill of receiving praise from your peers.

Obviously this can be a controversial topic. The nature of how to give, what to give, and whether or not you are supposed to benefit has been argued by sages and everyday people alike for thousands of years. It is one of those topics that is likely never to be solved to everyone's satisfaction. We simply have to content ourselves with what we find works best for each of us.

What would be worse, I imagine, is if someone were to simply forgo this essential step because he or she cannot stop thinking of the benefits to him- or herself. In this case it would be much better for everyone concerned if this hypothetical person would follow the old Nike advertisement and "Just Do It." Just as we do not want to create a generation of self-aggrandizing braggarts, we also do not want people so fearful of their own egos that they stop doing anything.

Deciding on which organization or group of organizations deserve your donations of time and money can be challenging. The first challenge is that there are an astonishing number of charitable organizations. Compounding that is the number of for-profit groups that seek volunteers, such as for the position of greeter in some popular big-box retail establishments. Some people also choose to support political campaigns and other causes that do not directly help others, but which they believe will eventually lead to the betterment of our society.

The second challenge is that there seem to be multiple organizations for every cause. As much as you desire to help them all, it would be physically impossible to do so.

Regarding the first challenge, it is important to sit down and figure out exactly which causes you would like to help. This can be anything from helping homeless people or homeless animals to providing food for refugees or supporting an entire at-risk nation. Perhaps you have an overwhelming desire to become a greeter or make political phone calls for a certain candidate. Whatever your favorite causes, for now just try to focus on one or two that you feel are most important.

The second challenge is much harder to solve but is not impossible either. The best place to start is to ask people you trust which organizations they believe are helping the most in the cause you would like to support. You can do a simple web search on these organizations and get a pretty basic feel for their trustworthiness as well. If your company has any ties with charitable organizations, that is a good place to start since your company might match your personal donation.

Now that you have decided on which organization to support, it is a good idea to contact it in some manner. If there is a website, check to see if it has an online donation or volunteer sign-p form. If not, check for the group's postal address or phone number. If you like the organization enough to continue supporting it, try to establish a regular contact within the organization to help you coordinate your efforts.

Once you get the hang of it, you will probably find many other groups you would like to help with your time and money as well. This is a very good chain reaction to experience and one that will lead to a very blessed life indeed.

Chapter 5

Create

When we use our energy to create new things we are becoming part of the very same energy that created this world. We are using the knowledge gained by humans when we were given a touch of the divine spark. If we were made by the ultimate creator in that creator's image, then we by our very nature are also master creators.

Creating can mean so many different things. The very act of being creative is inherent in us all, and each of us has been given a unique gift or skill to create with. The best way to find out where your creative gift lies is to see where you most enjoy being creative. If you find yourself desiring to paint, then that is likely where you should direct your creative energies. Your first work will probably not be a masterpiece; but if you found yourself enjoying what you were doing all the same, you are probably on the right path.

This book represents my desire to create, and writing is the medium I most enjoy. I do like to paint and have a musical background as well, but when I feel the need to express myself the most I invariably do it through writing. I am not writing this book for critics, nor do I have any specific reader in mind. I certainly am not writing it out of a desire for wealth but as a means to be more creative in my everyday life.

While creating, it is extremely important that you disregard what other people think of your work. You are the one creating that piece of work, and you need only pay attention to your desire and your divine inspiration. Whatever the art critic, music fan, or book reviewer thinks is immaterial to you in the moment of creation. Of course nearly all creative people will have others who disagree with their work or compare it to others. As the American author Elbert Hubbard so aptly put it, "To avoid criticism do nothing, say nothing, be nothing."

Obviously we were not put here on this Earth to be nothing. That would be a waste of time and space for everybody and everything. You are meant to be somebody, do something, and get your message heard. This means that you will be criticized from time to time. You will be a much greater person for gaining the ability to ignore this criticism and create nonetheless.

Every time you create, you are adding to the magic of this world. You are stepping out of the realm of the consumer and into that of the producer. While there is nothing wrong with being a consumer, a truly blessed life consists of also being a producer. You cannot truly understand the magic that we as humans are capable of without pulling from yourself, your imagination, and your divine connection to Source itself an act of beauty that has never been seen before.

Even if what you produce is a dance that nobody but you will ever see, a song that is for your ears alone, or poetry that hides on a dusty bookshelf in your back room forever, you are still contributing to the world at large. You know what you have produced, and your art is not diminished in any way for its small audience.

Of course the only reason why your dance, song, or poetry would have such a small audience is because you choose not to display it to the world. This is much to the world's dismay because, regardless of what you feel may be the quality of your work, I can assure you that at least one other person will learn something from what you have produced. That person will be changed in a subtle way and will likewise change everything he or she does and everyone he or she touches in a subtle way as a result of what you have taught him or her.

Our society is the way it is because of the people who live in it. The simplest way to change our society is to change the people who live in it. Your art, in whatever capacity or at whatever skill level, has that ability to change people. The very act of creation forces a change upon all of us in ways that we cannot yet imagine, until we are exposed to all of the wondrous creations that you have yet to come up with.

Creating also has the wonderful side benefit of making you more tolerant of other people's creations. Having gone through the difficult beginning period when your skill does not quite match up with your vision or ambition, you will be much more understanding when you hear a neighbor painfully coaxing notes out of a brand new violin. Similarly you may find yourself taking more of an interest in cultural and artistic offerings in your surrounding community. This has the added benefit of supporting your fellow creators and helps bring about a more enlightened society.

Certainly you will still find some art you cannot identify with in any way, but chances are that you will not shy away from it nearly as much as someone who never creates. You will at least look at that sculpture, listen to that song, or watch that dance to see what, if anything, you may learn from it. While there is no guarantee that you will learn anything from this particular piece of art, at least you tried before dismissing it out of hand.

This brings you into community with your fellow artists, people who can inspire you to create at new levels and far more frequently than you thought possible before.

Sometimes the hardest part about creating is coming up with an idea. I can certainly identify with this. In my much younger days, I played bass guitar for a small Dixie jazz band in Southern California. When we played some of our small gigs around town, I found something out about myself: while I could play almost any piece of music someone set in front of me, I could not improvise to save my life.

I could parrot other people's expression and art, but despite my training I was unable to come up with a single original musical idea. My life was far from perfect at the time, and I had a lot that needed expressing. But I simply could not imagine where to start. I needed divine inspiration.

Someone very near and dear to my heart taught me that one of the best ways to reach that divine inspiration is in the form of dreams. At that point in my life, I hadn't thought much about dreams, and I almost never remembered them. When this person taught me some very simple techniques for dream recall and how to experience more vivid dreaming, the ideas started coming at me faster than I could implement them.

I have made it a point to always act on those ideas in my dreams, as I have come to believe that those ideas are not mine alone. They belong to our divine creator. Just as I would not want someone to squander whatever good idea I imparted to him or her, I similarly do not want to waste any inspiration that is given to me in a dream.

Once you have decided upon your desired means of expressing yourself and have come up with a great idea, it is time to implement it. Set aside enough time each day to work on your creation. This is key because momentum is a very important part of the creative process. You must not let yourself get sidetracked for too long or, like a swimmer away from the pool for an extended period, you will have a long road back to where you started.

It is inconceivable that you do not have at least a few minutes each day to dedicate to your creation. Regardless of how busy your life is, how many pulls on your time you already have, there is something you can set aside for five minutes. By saying that you have no time to create, you are essentially saying that every single little thing you do throughout your day is more important than yourself. That is simply not right. Even if you never watch one minute of television, do not have an Internet connection to waste time on, and have absolutely no interest in reading a newspaper, you still have small tasks that can be temporarily set aside.

My grandmother is particularly fond of telling me that a page a day makes a book in a year. This is very true and would also lead to a pretty long book. What this little gem of wisdom also does is illustrate the power of persistence. If you were to take a few minutes out of each day for your creative works, you would not only fall into a wonderful habit of continual creation but you would also accomplish a rather large body of work in a relatively short period of time.

Just think of how many books, paintings, songs, sculptures, or whatever you could have created had you started this practice earlier in your life. Now I certainly do not want you to start lamenting your past and any potentially wasted opportunities. That would not serve any useful purpose. I would ask, though, for you to hold onto that feeling and imagine life ten years from now if you started today. How would it feel to have written ten books or displayed ten works of art? Picture that wonderful feeling of accomplishment and hold onto the vision.

This step is especially applicable to children. If you could teach them to put as much time into expressing themselves creatively as they put into homework or playing *World of Warcraft*, they will be much happier and well off the rest of their lives. While it is not too late to start these practices as an adult, the effect of starting young can be dramatic.

Too many times a so-called troubled youth is just another person who needs to express him- or herself but has neither the wisdom nor the experience to know how to do that. You can help this young person by showing him or her that it is okay to create art in all of its many splendors. You can make this world more artistic and magical by being a wonderful example to your children.

Chapter 6

Work

Much like the topic of exercise, the topic of work usually does not excite most people. They imagine trudging through another day at the office, another early morning line at the factory, or another day answering silly questions behind a cash register. While these are all examples of work with their respective joys and pitfalls, the idea of any sort of work is preferable to the idea of no work at all.

We are all familiar with the old saying, "All work and no play makes Jack a dull boy." This is true, but you could also say, "All play and no work makes Jack an unfulfilled boy." Humans have such a desire to work, to make our contribution to society that when we stop doing so our health can suffer. The reason why some people actually seek out unemployment is a mystery to many ordinary people and politicos alike. It is this universal desire to work that makes the very idea of welfare such a persistently controversial topic.

We simply have a hard time respecting those people whom we feel do not contribute.

The truth lies somewhere in between. The vast majority of people on welfare are not there out of laziness or a lack of desire to contribute but for reasons beyond their control. It is for these people that the social services exist and must continue to exist. If people were not ever given a second chance, ours would not be much of a society.

The idea of work persists, and I include this chapter for those who do not enjoy their work or even the very idea of it. Usually the problem lies not with the work or even the person doing the work, but the person and the work are a bad combination.

If you do not enjoy what you do for a living, you are simply doing the wrong thing. If you think all work is bad, boring, and to be avoided, you have never found the right type of work for you. It is a very simple fact that if you enjoy what you are doing, you will enjoy work.

The first step toward finding what you want to do is to change your mind about a lot of preconceptions we have taken as truth in our modern capitalist society.

The first preconception to squash is that some jobs are better than others. Yes, of course, some jobs pay more than others. Yes, some jobs are safer than others. And yes, some jobs just aren't even pleasant to consider. However, it is important to remember that you are not every person. You are individual in your tastes, desires, and values.

Not everyone wants the pressure a high-paying job comes with. Not everyone wants a safe, boring desk job. Not everyone considers a dirty job unappealing. You have been sold this idea that you cannot be happy unless you are wearing a tie and earning a six-figure salary. While that can certainly please some people, it is not for everyone.

A person who is content with the comparatively simple life of janitorial duties would find office politics repugnant and impossible to grasp. Someone whose biggest concern is how the weather will affect his or her crops would be horrified to see the backroom bargaining that is the futures market. You do not have to work at a job you do not like, and you do not have to leave a job you enjoy because other people think poorly of it.

I understand the perspective of thinking that if only you earned more money your problems would disappear. Believe me I have been there many times. That does not make it true, however. There are many people today who earn astonishingly large amounts of money who would be much happier farming or waiting tables. There is honesty in manual labor that can be hard to come by in the corporate world.

Then again there are people who are genuinely meant to be in that office space, people working jobs below their skill level who do need to get out and move up. Some people's ambitions are far too high for simple work. These people would no more enjoy selling gadgets at an electronics store than the farmer would enjoy the trading floor of the New York Stock Exchange.

We were all put here on this Earth to do something, but what is the best way to find out what that something is? Find out what you enjoy. Think back to what you wanted to be when you were a kid, what you used to imagine your work life to be when you were in high school. Do not think about your personal life or the home you always wanted. For this exercise simply think back to what you thought you would be doing for a living.

Now that you remember what you wanted to do, think of it in terms of what you know that job to entail now. You have undoubtedly met people who hold that position. What did you think of them? Do they have personalities you could get along with, or were they the type of people you would want to avoid? Could you imagine working for or with these people?

If you were unable to come up with anything in the previous exercise, then I am afraid I have some terribly good news for you. The chances are high that you are supposed to work for yourself. Entrepreneurial tendencies are natural and used to be very much the norm in our society.

Before the days of megacorporations and big-box retail chains, there were Main Streets filled with family-owned businesses. We may think of these barber shops, general stores, and antique dealers as something gone from the landscape of our Western society, but they were simply people who for one reason or another decided to start home based businesses. They haven't disappeared but have changed their scope. Unfortunately in this modern world of chains and conglomerates, there isn't much room for the old Main Street; but there is still a lot of room for private businesses without physical shops.

Of course I am not talking about those types of businesses you see in the backs of magazines, advertising that you can work for yourself for five thousand dollars a week stuffing envelopes. In my opinion having an upline or sponsor is not the same as having your own business.

No, the type of business I am talking about is something that you truly believe in and take pleasure in doing. Perhaps it is a franchise or something the world has never seen before. Maybe it is as simple as setting up an online store to sell books and your own artwork. The sky is the limit.

Remember that a bored life is not a blessed life, and you are not serving anyone by continuing to perform a job you do not like. The money is not worth the risk to your mental, physical, or spiritual health. If you are not enjoying your work, then it is time to start looking for work you will enjoy. There is work that is right for you.

Work does not only apply to what we do for a living. There is work all around us that needs to be done, however a great many people choose to avoid that work by any means possible. While you may find it more enjoyable to watch television than do the dishes or vacuum, you will find it much more enjoyable to watch that television show once you have tended to those minor chores. There is nothing that can sap the fun out of leisure time like some trivial chore hanging over your head. By tending to the chores first and then enjoying yourself, you will achieve more peace in your life.

If you have been the type of person who avoids these types of mundane tasks, you will pleasantly surprise those around you. The thing about work is that it needs to be done. If you are not the one doing it, then someone else has to do your share.

This is not really fair. Perhaps you have someone in your life that is more than happy to look after you like that; but it would be a tremendous blessing, courtesy, and act of love if you were to help him or her for a change.

I am not trying to make anyone feel bad, but without work we are not living life to the fullest. I know this firsthand. I used to make it a regular game to see how much housework I could get out of doing. I would have much rather browsed the Internet or watched television than do the dishes.

However, the time comes for all of us when we are the only ones around to do these sorts of things, and what I found is that television or computer gaming was never as relaxing and enjoyable until after I finished cleaning up. It is only when we appreciate work in all its various forms that our leisure time has any meaning. We cannot live that blissed-out, hammock-on-the-beach, blessed existence in good conscience if we do not know what an honest day's work feels like. As with all the other steps, the more you work the more you will learn to appreciate it.

Chapter 7

Visualize

Reading the name of this step, you might ask, "What does visualize mean?" If you have spent any time with members of the New Age community, you may have heard this term quite a bit; but perhaps you are still not sure what it means exactly.

Visualizing is simply a way of seeing something that you would like to have happen or want to acquire in your mind's eye. When you sit back and imagine something, that is a type of visualization.

Visualization is an important practice is because, when we know exactly what we want, we are more likely to achieve our goal. Visualizing gives you a picture of something to work toward on a physical, mental, and spiritual level. In my book *Angels of Abundance*, I explain how the universe works like a diner with an endless menu. You can have anything you want with the caveat that you will receive exactly what you ask for.

This is great news if you know what you want. If, on the other hand, you accidently order something that ends up being unappealing, you will still receive it. Visualizing helps us order only what we want and leaves out all the potentially yucky stuff.

Visualizing is the easiest step in this book. You only have to sit back, relax, and see something you would like to work toward. It does help, particularly if you are actively trying to manifest this item spiritually, if you can see this item or end result in as much clarity and detail as possible. This detail helps anchor your mind on the idea so that you are not ordering something you have no desire for.

Visualization will help you lead a more blessed life because you will increasingly feel as if you are making concrete goals and, more importantly, achieving them. The most important step in any journey is to find out where you are going. Visualizing gives you a road map to your future.

You will, of course, still make your own choices about what to visualize and how you mean to obtain what you see. You have many options.

Those of you who are more spiritually inclined may feel that you simply want to manifest this piece of abundance. The more right-brained readers will be able to formulate a plan that has this object as its end goal. At the very least, once you become a skilled visualizer, you will be able to essentially see into the future and decide if this is something you even want in the first place.

The primary thing we are seeking to avoid by visualizing is living in the past. A life of regrets is not a blessed life. When you visualize what you would like to achieve, you are ensuring that you will have no regrets. There will still be circumstances that are beyond your control and things will occur that you may wish had never happened. But if it is within your power to change something, you will be able to.

You may wonder how on earth simply imagining things could cause them to come into being. Keep in mind that every crazy idea, invention, and movement was once just a figment of someone's imagination. Albert Einstein said that imagination is more important than knowledge. This is often true.

If you want to achieve something, whether it is buying a new car or getting a promotion at work, you must be able to imagine it first. It is only those ideas that we close off from ourselves and dare not risk even imagining that are beyond our reach. Anything you can visualize and truly believe you can do, you can.

This technique is widely used among athletes. They are regularly encouraged by coaches, managers, and teammates to imagine winning the game, see themselves making that shot. The players who practice this skill the most have gone on to become some of the most celebrated athletes in history.

Have you ever known someone who was so convinced that he or she was going to achieve something that you had no doubt about his or her being right? This person was so confident that expecting anything but success for him or her seemed ludicrous. That is visualization at its most powerful.

We leave this step with this final thought: If you can visualize, you can see into the future. It is your choice to decide if that is a future you want for yourself or not. If you can see a goal, you can reach it.

Chapter 8

Relax

I know, I know…first I tell you to work and now I tell you to relax. Actually these two topics go hand in hand. You cannot have one without the other. As we touched on in the previous chapter, relaxation without work is a very unfulfilling and potentially stressful endeavor. Likewise work without relaxation is exhausting and potentially miserable.

The relationship between work and relaxation is instinctual in all creatures. The extremes go from the nearly ever-working ants to members of the cat family, who seem content to sleep twenty hours a day. Fortunately we humans fall somewhere in the middle. We neither want to toil all day every day, nor do we get much satisfaction out of sleeping the day away. However, an increasingly large number of people seem to be going the way of the ant.

The technology we have available to us today is remarkable in many ways. It allows many of us to work from home. It also allows more and more people to break away from the corporate world and own their own businesses, if only part time.

In this world of 3G signals and ubiquitous Wi-Fi hot spots, we are able to work almost anywhere. The downside, of course, is that we tend to work wherever we go. No longer is the park or the beach a safe sanctuary from our professions. These places have become like second offices, resulting in many people choosing to extend the work day much more than they used to.

It is not only individuals who are using this technology to push themselves to ever-stretching work hours. Corporate management takes advantage of the situation as well. Since nearly everyone has an Internet connection at home and even in his or her pocket with a smartphone, managers are not shy about e-mailing off-duty employees to help out with some off-site work. These requests are natural and to be expected, nothing more than human nature.

However, without taking these much-needed spaces of time away from work to genuinely relax, we are in effect squandering all our efforts. Certainly you could get much more done in a shorter period of time if you never stopped working, but how much less work will you accomplish over your lifetime if you burn yourself out? Nothing will bring you back to loving what you do for a living if you allow yourself or others to work you to the brink of exhaustion. At a certain point, you will have to relax.

The nature of relaxation and the various guises it comes in could fill an entire book by itself. I believe there is no such thing as invalid leisure time. Some people find television relaxing, others books or video games. Many people enjoy going out to bars or nightclubs. I even know one person who finds it particularly relaxing to chop firewood in his spare time.

Whatever you do it is important that you do it with your entire mind. This is not the time to check your e-mail. This is the time to do exactly what you want to do that has nothing to do with your profession. You should not feel guilty about it any more than you should be made to feel guilty about any other aspect of your life. You simply have to relax in order to be a productive member of society. A society that lacks any sort of recreation would resemble something out of the dystopian vision put forth by some of the classic mid-20th century writers.

It is a funny thing, this business of relaxing. There are so many areas of our society and economy that are based on nothing more than putting your feet up and relaxing with a nice hot cup of tea, or whatever other drink suits your fancy. However, there is still this shame or stigma surrounding our desire and requirement for downtime. Some people call it loafing or goldbricking; others call it goofing off or living in a dream. I call it investing in yourself and your livelihood.

The Jewish religion saw the need for people to stop working at least one day out of the week thousands of years ago. It was such an important and unmet need that it was made a critical part of the faith. This followed through to the two major subsets of that religion, Christianity and Islam. It is not hard to imagine a time when people were so used to working nonstop that, in order to have them simply take a day off, it had to be written into religious law.

Our society is not that far from this extreme. In fact we may be more workaholic in some cases than those ancient people were. It was not that long ago that you could drive down the highway at five o'clock on a Saturday or Sunday evening and have the place almost entirely to yourself. That is not the case these days. The daily commute knows no set weekend any longer, and anyone who is lucky enough to get both days of the weekend off is probably in business for him- or herself.

It doesn't matter what you do to unwind at the end of the day or during your vacation, so long as you make relaxing just as important to your life as working. We want you to be around for a very long time, long enough to really enjoy this blessed life that you are working on. Without a bit of relaxation, that can prove difficult indeed.

Chapter 9

Learn

One thing you can be very sure of throughout your life is that you will always have new opportunities to learn. We have such an abundance of learning material around us in the form of books, films, university classes, and the ancient art of lectures. You might even gain an astonishing amount of information by having a conversation with friends over coffee.

At some point, however, many people feel they have learned enough and simply stop seeking knowledge. This is a mistake because cutting off the flow of knowledge is akin to saying there are no new people, ideas, or technology coming along in the world. This is of course ludicrous. Learning to enjoy learning opens you up to many exciting new prospects and lets you continue being a critical part of this world and its affairs.

Not everything you learn will be useful, however, because not all information is true or relevant. You can read the front page of the newspaper right now and learn all sorts of fascinating things about the town you currently live in, but I can almost guarantee that you are better off not gaining that sort of knowledge.

Not every story on that front page is made up, but nearly all stories are sensationalized or included for their shock value, so they are basically useless to you. Similarly whatever information you would glean from one of the ever-increasing number of twenty-four-hour television news stations would be so sensationalized and biased as to be completely irrelevant. Believe me; none of us need to learn how to become angrier.

No, the type of learning we are discussing here can help you improve your life and the world around you in some way, no matter how small. Learning a new art is very high on that list and something I encourage wholeheartedly, but it does not have to start or stop there.

Because we live in such a productive society, some truly great people do not stop their work even after retirement. It is possible to go to nearly any night school, community college, or correspondence institute and learn at the proverbial feet of former captains of industry, commercial farmers, and world-class artists. We are blessed to be in a time when people can pass on in such varied ways the wisdom and lessons they learned after years in one industry.

While there is nothing wrong with learning from a traditional teacher, the fact that people can teach based on their life experience and not their teaching credentials is a gift to be utilized. If you are interested in learning a specialized field, who better to consult than a specialist in that field?

You wonder how you can find it enjoyable to learn. Perhaps the joy of learning left you long ago in college, high school, or even grade school. This is understandable and something I can identify with. However, if you have read this far into the book, I can assure you that the answer will not surprise you. The answer, of course, is that you will find it enjoyable to learn if you learn about something you enjoy.

If you find math tedious, you probably should not sign up for that advanced calculus night course. If you cannot stand getting your hands dirty, the local gardening group is not for you.

Find what you are interested in and learn more about it.

Learning, like all other aspects of our lives, is much more fulfilling and effective when we enjoy what we are doing. There are times when we must study subjects we have no interest in, but usually that happens only when we are being trained in school or in our careers.

Learning also has the side benefit of getting you out and meeting new people. Even if you are taking online classes at your local community college, you are still interacting with people you otherwise would never have met. Some of the most fascinating people can be found in these online adult education classes, and you will be much better off for having known them.

The chance for business networking is also quite high, especially if you are studying something that you intend to make a business out of. If you are planning on starting your own business, the people you meet in a small-business management class can become invaluable later on when you are getting established. Likewise if you are simply learning about your favorite hobby, you will be able to meet like-minded people from your community.

Learning is a lifelong process that should never really stop. It can keep your brain sharp and focused in your later years and intellectually stimulated your entire life. Just as you would find it hard to live a balanced and blessed life without any sort of physical activity or spiritual expression, you should not ignore intellectual stimulation either.

Chapter 10

Socialize

As the English poet John Donne said, "No man is an island." Humans are social creatures by nature, and we instinctively crave social interaction with our peers. In this age of Internet shopping and telecommuting, it is easier than ever to have nothing to do with your fellow human beings. Rather than this being something to revel in and cultivate, we must start taking steps to ensure that we do not isolate ourselves too much.

Fifty years ago, socialization was something that happened as a matter of course. You could not mail a letter, buy orange juice, or even take a walk without interacting with your neighbors and other members of your community. It was very common at that time to know all of your neighbors' names, as well as those of their children, your mail carrier, and the milkman.

Back then it was possible in more densely populated places to order your groceries over the telephone, all your clothing from mail order catalogs, and other such things; but for the most part those were the exceptions rather than the rule.

Take this book, for example. How did you come across it? Chances are that you are familiar either with my work or one of my family member's work and learned that this book was due for release. In most cases it took a simple search on Amazon.com or Barnes & Noble to find out that the book can be purchased in either paperback or downloadable form, and a few clicks later it was on its merry way to your house. That is a very efficient delivery system and one most authors and readers are grateful for.

However, let's take a step back in time to the arbitrarily selected year of 1959. In 1959 you most likely would have heard about the book from a friend, who had heard about it from another friend. Or perhaps you were browsing for new nonfiction in the library, at the corner newsstand, or in a bookstore and the picture on the front of the book caught your eye. A quick inquiry to the shopkeeper or librarian would have let you know the book's availability and popularity. Going to and from these establishments as well as the entire time you would have spent looking at books, you would have been in an almost constant state of socialization.

Of course we still have libraries, newsstands, and bookstores; but a quick check of the balance sheet for most bookstores and the dramatically reduced operating hours for libraries all over the world are proof that these establishments are a vanishing breed. And if they go, so go some of our opportunities to socialize. Since the beginning of time, unless one chose to become a hermit, there really was not a lot of choice but to socialize. The amount of human interaction was just enough for some people, too much for others, and far too little for still others. Humans are creatures of habit, though, and we seem to have an almost hive consciousness. We remember on an instinctual level that we are meant to have more interaction with our fellow man than we do right now.

Think back to when you were a child. Chances are you were involved in sports or social groups. While not all of us enjoyed this sort of thing, I am reasonably certain that all of us miss it from time to time because socialization is such a natural thing for children. There is no pretense behind it or any particular reason for it other than the existence of a group of children around the same age.

This social backbone of your life most certainly had troubles of its own, as children can be quite cruel to each other at times and for the most inexplicable reasons. However, the social ties you made then taught you more about how to interact with other humans than probably anything has since.

You can see this sort of interaction with adults— spontaneous and natural with only initial shyness and fear—but typically it is only during very specific events centered on sports or drinking. It is very rare, unless you are in some of the more gregarious countries of Europe and Australia that adults interact with strangers at restaurants, movie theaters, and even most stores.

This is the type of socialization that humans instinctively crave and are increasingly missing out on. This is also exactly the type of socialization we should all strive for to lead a more blessed life.

Fortunately it is easy to achieve this level of socialization if we recognize that it is something we want. Many people have already discovered this, forming book clubs, coffee groups, gardening clubs, and using a very popular website dedicated to meeting people with similar interests. These groups and people are there waiting for you; you simply have to take that next step and approach them.

I realize this can be daunting because one of the side effects of our sometimes isolated modern lives is that we have become shy. The more you interact with random people and groups, the more daring you become about approaching people. The reverse is also true. The more time you spend by yourself or in a very small social circle, the less daring you become.

Here are a few things to keep in mind when trying to get over that initial hurdle of introducing yourself or getting up the guts to join a group.

First, these are just people no different from you or me. They are not there to judge you and for the most part are probably very happy you have decided to interact with them. Since it is a social group, the members are probably socially oriented people, so any new member will be welcome.

Second, you have just as much to teach them as they have to teach you. Certainly you are going to learn a lot from these people, and chances are if you know them long enough they will help you with some important projects and events in your life. Likewise you know many things to share with these people and can become a great help to them throughout your relationship. You are not dependent on them any more than they are dependent on you, and you should not fear becoming beholden to them.

Third, this is not the only group available to you. If the chemistry between you and other members of the group is not there, you do not have to stay in an uncomfortable situation. You can move on to another group. There are nearly as many book clubs as there are books, so do not fear that you will have to put up with dominating personalities or other difficulties that would make you feel timid or cause you to think twice about interacting.

Finally, please keep in mind that this is not elementary school. These people are not going to go out of their way to be cruel to you simply because you are new. That sort of behavior rarely exists in the adult world and is not something you have to be afraid of.

In short you really do have nothing to fear and so much to gain. Social interaction is a necessity in our life and becomes more so the older we get. It is only through social interaction in a nonwork-related setting that we really get a picture of ourselves in relation to the world. Your friends and groups can help you become a better person and, through group action, bring about much more powerful change in the world.

Chapter 11

Dream

The study of dreams is massive in scope and can embody a great many subjects. I am lucky to be married to Melissa Virtue, a wonderful teacher and lifelong student of dreams. From her I have learned the power of dreams. However, the dreams we are discussing for this final simple step are not the type that come to us when we sleep.

The type of dreaming I refer to here is akin to visualization and affirmations. It is knowing that you want more out of life and making it your focus to achieve that goal. This is the type of dreaming done by Einstein, Hughes, Bell, Gates, and Jobs. This is the ever-present desire to invent, create, and improve your life and the lives of everybody in the world.

We all dream, especially when we are quite young. We imagine how we are going to come up with the next great invention, the great American novel, or the next blockbuster movie.

We are so sure that we will accomplish these things that we never stop to think how we will do so. This is a truly magical thing that we must strive to never lose or, if lost, to regain immediately.

Once upon a time it was considered a bad thing to be called a dreamer. A dreamer was considered idealistic, impractical, and not likely to hold down a regular job with a steady paycheck. This would have been someone to avoid when deciding whom to marry and someone who would be quickly redistributed in the work force.

Today we have fortunately started to change that view dramatically. We live in the time of the instant millionaire, who with daring bravado ignores all criticism and so-called common sense to think outside the box and change everyone's lives.

Once again I ask you to consider how you obtained this book. If you turned on your computer, fired up your web browser, and purchased it at an online store, you have just proven over a dozen crazy dreamers right and untold hundreds of naysayers wrong.

If you had told the average person in 1965 that you were going to use your computer to make the bulk of your purchases, he or she would have considered you mad. And that person would have been right if such a string of dreamers had not been born in such a short period of time.

Every single one of us has this same potential within us. Each of us throughout our life has had and will have again one of these game-changing moments of inspiration. The only difference between the people we read about in the newspaper and the rest of us is that they acted on their dreams.

History has shown that no idea can be too crazy, no idea so well established that it cannot be changed, and no industry so perfect that it cannot be revolutionized by one strong individual with the knowledge to do it better.

This is the final step because it combines with the previous ten to help you live a blessed life. By integrating the rest of the steps into your life and following your dreams, you will have the life you have always wanted. You may dream all you want, but without the previous steps there is much less chance that anything will come of your dreams. Likewise without dreaming you will find several of the previous steps difficult.

You can be the person you have always wanted to be and live the life you have always wanted. You are a wonderful dreamer possessed of the most life-changing ideas. Keep those dreams alive at all costs, and constantly work toward achieving them.

Never worry that your dreams are impractical or that you may not be able to afford to see them come to light. Your ideas are given to you precisely because they can be achieved by you with enough perseverance. The universe is more than capable and willing to provide you all of the abundance and people you need to see your project through to completion. This project need not be judged by others, as the true usefulness of your creation will be obvious to all once you complete it.

There are no more interesting people on this planet than the dreamers. Let me be more specific: there are no more interesting people on this planet than those who allow themselves to dream. These dreams are what keep a person going and provide the continuing and remarkable achievements of the human race.

Separate yourself from those who have given up their dreams with no intention of picking them back up again. Join the ranks of the leaders of the world and dream as big as you can imagine. I and the rest of the world thank you in advance.

Chapter 12

Thoughts on Perspective

If you have made it this far without skipping ahead, then you have gained a lot of insight into my life and how I try to live it. Depending on how you heard about this book, you may be familiar with my family and our literary legacy. Often over the years, I have been asked what it was like to live with such prolific writers and teachers. This book is my answer.

Obviously everybody will skip some of these steps some of the time. I know I do. However, they do represent a bare minimum of what we should at least attempt in our lives. This business of living a blessed life is one that every single person instinctually knows how to do but for one reason or another has forgotten. I am not blessed with a particularly sharp insight that is unavailable to anyone else, and certainly my family legacy does not give me wisdom above and beyond the next person's. I am simply trying to remember this blessed life that I contracted before coming down to the planet, and in remembering I am hoping to share it with at least one other person.

I have kept this book intentionally short because these ideas are not radical ones. I do not attempt to convince you of anything other than your own potential. It is not my desire to talk you into any idea you may find repulsive or contrary to your view. I only want to show you that you have nothing to fear and everything to gain by living your life exactly the way you have always wanted to.

I am aware that some of my views can be controversial, however subscribing to all of them is not a requirement for following any of these steps. I will conclude with the subject I find especially important for you to keep in mind with these sorts of books and activities: perspective.

Perspective is defined as a particular evaluation of a situation or facts, especially from one person's point of view. This may strike you as an odd inclusion for the final part of this book because you probably assume your point of view is something you cannot control. Actually perspective is something you can control, however it takes self-control and discipline to do so.

To show you how to gain perspective and use it wisely, I must first illustrate how to lose perspective. Perspective can be lost by allowing yourself to become part of a cause rather than its becoming a part of you.

For example, let us say that a certain man registers to vote for a particular political party. Perhaps his parents or friends vote for that party, and he feels a kinship to it. Or perhaps he read the party's mission statement and decided it fits his ideology closest. Regardless of how the decision came about, he decided to vote that way and the matter is settled.

In the lead-up to the next election, however, he starts hearing on radio or television several of the party's candidates making impassioned speeches about the evils that would befall this country if the rival party were to win. Further he reads in newspaper articles and party pamphlets that the party's opinions about how to solve the nation's problems are so obvious that only a crazy person could think anything else would work.

Foolishly the man starts believing the propaganda and rhetoric, joining in a protest or a march on the state capital or starting a letter-writing campaign to swing voters admonishing them to vote the proper way. Perhaps he even starts comparing his chosen party to rebel groups from our nation's past. If you were to suggest to him that there might be another way to look at things and more than one way to solve a problem, he would likely react with disbelief and anger.

That is a man who has lost perspective. He bought into what other people were saying and let the propaganda machine roll right over him. At no point did he stop to listen to the other side or look at the exact issues and formulate his own opinion. He let himself become a part of that party, rather than letting the party become a part of him. This is a rather extreme and somewhat facetious example, of course, but one that does seem to be happening more and more.

Losing perspective is not exclusive to the realm of politics. Living too long in a large city or a very powerful nation without traveling or moving around too often causes people to lose perspective as well. In those cases people develop tunnel vision because they are absolutely unaware and uninterested in what happens outside their city or nation.

Likewise, people who embrace one activity to too large of a degree risk losing perspective. It can be easy to figure that life consists of nothing but lifting weights or throwing footballs if that is all you do every day and all you talk about every night.

The key to gaining perspective is to keep a realistic view of the world. You must recognize that this world is full of incredibly diverse people, most of who are not like you and do not share your interests. When your political party loses a race or your sports team does not come in first, you may be disappointed; but it is not the end of the world. You need to recognize that there will be other activities in the future just as important to you and that other people have their own ideas of what is important.

Throughout your journey with all the steps in this book, it is equally important not to lose perspective. Certainly your exercise is important, as are your faith, community, work, and hobbies. However, we must all strive continuously to keep our perspective broad and not let these activities define who we are.

You have within you the divine spark of the creator, and that is more important than anything you can ever do or anyone else can ever say.

Thank you for your time,

Grant Virtue

About the Author

Grant Virtue is a fifth-generation metaphysician, who has studied candle magic and music theory throughout his life. He is the technical coordinator for Angel University, and he plays and records meditation music. Grant currently lives on the Big Island of Hawaii with his wife, Melissa, and their cat, Pepper.

Website: www.GrantVirtue.com
Twitter: @GrantVirtue

Also by Grant Virtue

Angel Words: Visual Evidence of How Words can be Angels in Your Life

Angel Blessings Candle Kit

Available from Hay House, Inc.

www.hayhouse.com